T0156995

Other books by Scott Byorum:

The A.M. God
Dooley Downs

TRIDENT

Scott Byorum

www.trafford.com

North America & international
toll-free: 1 888 232 4444 (USA & Canada)
fax: 812 355 4082

Contents

To everyone I've ever known and to myself. Life is like a Trident, piercing deeply into your Heart, your Soul, and your Mind.

"We are what we think about all day long."
~ Ralph Waldo Emerson

Take time each day
To play outside in the fresh air
And roller skate
Jump rope
Look up
You might see a pretty butterfly
A bird
Or a cloud in the sky
~ written by my Grandmother Ruth Andersen

§BLUE§

"…promise you won't forget about me, ever. Not even when I'm a hundred…"
~ **Christopher Robbin (A.A. Milne)**

Wind in the Mustard

Wind aboard the bushy trees
On a morning warmly scented sweet
Hope to hear your awakening
Nestled in the breeze

Wind in the mustard field
Such a luscious lonely sight
Hope you make it back to me
On any other night

Wind upon the shutter boards
Clacking against the weathered panes
Hope to see you walking down
That darkly graveled lane

Wind sleeks through a carnival
Brilliant baubles besiege the eye
Strapped upon the carousel
Horses prance and bray
In picture perfect still life
A part of this is eternal
Surely I should see you there
Where the shadows set your eyes aglow
Amidst straw and steel and flapping burlap
Where the wind engulfs your skin
Your hair and dress play sweet distress
And your touch still feeds the flame
I'm glad you came

Wind within the willows
Hauntingly
Calls your name

Wildflower

Grow wildflower
Grow
In fragrant fields so sweet with rain
The swollen ground to sprout your mane
It feeds you from below
Wildflower
Grow

Blow wildflower
Blow
In rushing fields that dance and sway
Unto the wind your colors play
The Sun's warmth swift in tow
Wildflower
Blow

Roam wildflower
Roam
Let the shallow air become your senses
Despite the whitewashed prowling fences
Where birds have not yet flown
Wildflower
Roam

Where Destiny Resides

Behind the door of intuition
Where spinning jesters clad in checkerboard fabrics
Sound brass trumpets
And float in universal symmetry
In the hall of Christmas checkered tiles
Lies an open study
Garbed in mahogany and rich wove cloth
Where an elaborate marble fireplace
Burns warm and bright
In a high-backed chair
With an open book upon his lap
Rests a weary old man
Spent but strangely fulfilled

I sit quietly there
Within my age
And purchase no more fear

When

When the only thing whirling around me
Is the dust in the breeze
The whispering of leaves
And the laden sigh
Deep with strength and ease
Yet somehow melancholy
Of an ancient wistful sea

When the only people places things in my life
Are the rampant spools
Of recorded imagery and sound
Replaying themselves over and over again
Behind and before my waking eyes
Blindingly all around
As each moment is stored in full within

When my heart borders on the disparity of random conditions
Brooding indolently
Musing in sentiment and longing
Pumping pitifully with disease of sorrow
Welling distant oceans of salty tears into my eyes
They threaten to plummet
But always manage to evaporate
Before tracing down my flushed and worried skin

When desolation weeds through my worn and weathered structure
Washing away with time and testament
The fancies of a dying age
The frailty of a lying face
In measurements too subtle to be seen
When with chaotic naivety
Of all things are eventually replaced

When what goes on out there
Is so far away
Alien to what is here
Unrecognizable and empty of pattern
Useless to word or to pen or to capture
Waning from sight and from sound and from rapture
When nothing really known bears truth

My thoughts turn to you

Up Here

Up there
Up there in the cosmos
It's cold
Empty and cold
Only intermittent lightning bugs disturb the all consuming reign
Of the vast icy waste before me
The limitless vacuum
Of space
Those fathomless congregations of swirling fireflies
Colligate and divorce on a scale too massive to witness
A scale that makes my existence
Seem infinitesimal
A figment
A blink
And it is
As is the gnat or the germ to me

So I think that all things must have a place
A purpose
A function
Some kind of space
Not manifest
Or preordained by an ultimate higher source
Just interaction
Blatant or subtle
Inconsequential or profound
It is all the same
Just survival
And death
And life
I think of these things
Within my limited time my limited space
As minimal as that may be

Up here
Up here in the cosmos
Up here
So far above that awesome blue ball that I once called home
That I once felt was my very own
With its powdery swirling atmosphere
And its scabbed and scaly patches
I float
I float above it all
And think of my life
So trivial and insignificant
Negligible to its grandeur
As it must be to space
I float
Up here
I float

Trajectory

As each heartbeat of the day
Whispers quietly away
And each passing of a year
Alleviates or solidifies your fears
As each hour at hand
Leads you further and farther
In both body and mind
From the womb towards the truth
Sail or stay
Set all others aside
Or fade away
But play
As you have always played
Your own music

Traffic

And they ran
Through the bold majestic tunnels
Howling like wolves
With their gnashing white teeth
And their penetrating grace
Their despairing black hair flowing in silken sheets behind them
Their feet fell like dancers
In a demonic ballet
Eyes smoldering like coals
Those eyes
Piercing
And they ran

To No Avail

All those memories
Those childhood whimsies
Those fanciful triumphs
All those recollections
Those embarrassing failures
Those dismal disappointments
All those shining moments
That seem to stick inside the melon rind
All those powerful passions
Those monumental first times
And all the magic moments thereafter
All the time involved
In learning to crawl
And eventually stand and walk
All those poignant talks
All those tribulations
Just to assimilate some purpose
All those moments of barely hanging on to what is real
And all that comes with ease
All the laughter
All the tears
The sad raking shivers
The screeching grating quivers
All that's been absorbed
Understood
And misinterpreted
All that's been ignored
Cast aside
Like so much petty waste
That one day returns in force
To sanctify or horrify
That one day twists your shape
All those people who've entered
And gone along their way
All who've stayed

All the miserable crap
All the generosity
All that's come to be
Is lost to him now...

He is once again a child
And his eyes stare blankly past the laminated postcard
Out and in to both realities
But locked in none
The simple blatant facts
The ugly brutal truth
Little is felt or understood
Despite the overwhelming transparency of the situation
The only sound
A sickeningly pathetic giggle
Escaping from a physically tormented maw
The contracted and contorted body twitching
To that ancient basic rhythm
All that time
To no avail

Thirteen

The light is too bright for my eyes
The light is too bright for my eyes
The light is too bright for my eyes

Prudence was the rich girl
Full of prideful lifeless struggle
Burning autumn leaves in fog drifts
Cooling warmth the flesh
So wistfully intelligent
So out of breath
No more breath
And it's dark in there
Foreboding and false
Much too dark to care
But her body bears capacity
It would take such persistent patience
To release the love in there

Little girl
Little girl
Lose your marbles
Little girl
Spill your senses on the floor
Spit and kick and scratch some more
Rant and rave and misbehave
Tantrum torn
Conscience worn
Face betrays the petty scorn
That resides behind the lies
Pinching up your eyes
Discovered

Little girl
Little girl
You've been discovered
Little girl
And your mouth is pursed in bitter curses
Brittle pages mark the verses
Where the only life you've ever led
Cascades around the past
The dead

Again again and on and on
You read the words the words are gone
All gone
Swallow deep and relish long
The sweet depression
The lonely song
Captured in the flowing dance
The need for need
The narrow lance
Seeping in as vines and creepers
Break away
Break away
Thirteen

The light is too bright for my eyes
The light is too bright for my eyes
The light is too bright for my eyes

The Slow Parade

Again the Asian Lady comes to me
Bathed in strands of ebony silk
She is ancient and wise
Weathered crossroads besiege her eyes
Countless men have fallen before her in blubbering shame
Their names disgraced
And yet she is slender and sleek
Youthful and sensuous
Men grovel on their knees before her
Groping her luscious body
Clawing away their dignity and pride
Only to mindlessly crawl
Crawl before her
Behold
She isn't there

But now she stands before me
In her mystical elegance
Her flowing black webs
She glares at me with understanding
And assured distaste
She fills my bottle
Like she fills my senses
But out there it is different
She knows that
With my back to the wall
My mind reels unsettled
Yet tired
Within the sweltering heat of the endless day
I watch the Slow Parade
Pass by

The Sad Little Boy

The sad little boy
Sits alone in the rye
With his knees tucked up
Past his chin
To his eyes
His innards twist in knots
And he really wants to cry
He sits and he rocks
And he tries
Tries
Tries

Crying spawns relief
Always dying feeds his grief
In the moments of a maelstrom
He could be flying in the breeze
Could be flying in the breeze

The sad little boy
Sits alone in the rye
The buzzards overhead
Circle high
Circle high

The Dead Years

"Memories will come to you
In time my boy
In time"
He aged 10 years before my eyes
Raised his weary head
And drained his cup of wine
And the caverns of his wrinkled face
Betrayed no hint
Of deep disgrace
His thoughts remained intact
But what of mine?
I asked him of forgotten years
When I was young
Naïve with fears
His delivered tongue drew pictures of romantic treasured tears
And his ancient withered hands crept up to greet his sullen smile
Pressed against his softened lips
Drew down to scratch his stubble chin
That remained throughout a lifetime
He leaned back into his chair
And I moved on

Tatterdemalion

She lay
So limp and empty
In my arms
In my arms

Scholar of delusion I was
Curled up inside a bottle of broken dreams
The sweet bitterness of candor
Waltzing drearily through my inner sanctum
Like two lovers dancing to a dirge of bland discord
And yet the candles are aflame
In our damply etched chamber
Washing their fragile persistence
Over dim and flickering shadows
That withdraw into the darker womb
The corners of this stony tomb

And now she lay in ravishing red
Laced in white and fineness
In my heart
In my heart

Stardust & Dreams

Sometimes the scenery slides past my eyes
Like so much stardust and dreams
And my head wanders high above it all
Aloft on clouds of rambling thoughts
Lifting by degrees

And sometimes reality rips through my sight
Magnified by folds
Crises and courage collide with my will
I'm called upon to speak my mind
My mouth trembles with such noise

And days may seem like weeks in some forgotten lonely hour
Eternity is but seconds in a daydream
Sometimes life is so short
That 80 years have come and passed by
And the only questions left are
Why?
Where did all the time go?
How much life did I live?
What did I leave in my wake?
What will happen to me now?

Seclusion

She stands there
Beyond that whipped and whispering
Tattered blanket of fog
That spreads its ragged tendrils
Through the thin and spiny branches
Of a darkly contorted tree
An odor of thick and musky moisture
Ranks heavy in the atmosphere
She stands over there

Revelry

I recall how the dead used to party
With powdery venom
And liquid tears
To release inhibitions
But which only served to galvanize their fears

I recall how the dead used to party
With bloodied lips
And blackened eyes
Ratty hair held their nested care
Pallid skin their sweet disguise

I recall how the dead used to party
Casting forth the ashen soot from their charcoal souls
Frozen in icy conversations
Self-absorbed with hate and loathing
Their heretic inclinations

I recall how the dead used to party
Emerging from their dreary cellars
As the burnt out evening gloom dimmed into night
They stalked the stony urban sidewalks
Unleashing granite smiles

I recall how the dead used to party
Masked in cold compassions
That veiled their warm conceit
But deep within their deadened hearts
Their dusty blood dribbles pitifully
Ebbing ever weaker
Time eating away at the inside
Capturing the causality of their casual actions
To flare like a furnace

At their final demise
And so with brief recognition
They pass away
From sight

Reunion

Breathe deep the smoke
Breathe deep the whispering tunes
Breathe deep the air that sets your hair aflame in the diminishing glare of
a sunset's searing fire
Your eyes ablaze
Your gaze afar
Wandering through fathomless blue pools of virgin desire

Now we talk
Now we laugh
Now we share these simple facts
These lingering faults
These basic feelings
That somewhere long ago
Were tucked neatly away in some remote recess of our minds

Now we walk to distant gleaming shores
What once was mine again is yours
What once was yours is free to me now
Like the wind
And your smile
A knowing grin

My eyes sparkle with the madness of it all

Yet it's not so strange
Even though it is
It's just right here
Us
Right here
Right now
Two familiar strangers
Sharing one another
Again
Anew

Quilt

What a filthy fabric we thread upon
Polluted with intangible designs
Dirty with deceit and tricky weavings
Tattered
And old
And though we've toiled long and hard in its creation
Working in the indelible patterns of its patchwork
Quilting its elusive shape to our liking
And taste
Laboring our fingers over its piano wire mesh
And its razor lined seams
And its barbed elaborations
Rarely does it ever comfort our slumber
Most often than not
It lies rumpled and soiled
Abused and disowned
Abandoned to some isolated crevice
In our deeply twisting minds
Until some savior
Makes it our own

Precipitation

Millions of raindrops
Here and there
Just a few
Here and there
The sky overcast
The trees in shadow
Just a few
Here and there

Numb

I want to be numb
Feel nothing
Have no inclinations
And no assumptions
I want to be vacant
Empty
Void
A hollow little boy
I want to have no one connecting me
With memories and feelings

I want to be blind
Thoughtless
Deaf and dumb
To all the world around me
And if given a chance
I'd like to crawl inside myself
And hide
Without sensation
Drifting off into quiet
Serene
Oblivion

Nerve

The thumping of a heartbeat
The beating of a drum
The ticking of a metronome
The tocking of a clock
The thocking of a woodpecker
The plunking water drops
The swishing windshield wipers
Slapping water to the rocks
The busy tone on telephones
When someone wants to talk
And if you have the time to spend
Thinking of it all
Remember me through years gone by
Don't even pause to call

More

You want more
And your lips peel back
More
And your face is wracked with
More
And your eyes flare up to
More
More
More More More

You want science
Science
Science offers answers
To questions
And questions to answers

You want objects
Objects
Objects occupy the space
You fill
Your house with

You want liquor
Liquor
And liquor makes you thicker
Much thicker
Than the liquor

You want a church
A church
A church that makes you hurt and speaks the words
You love
To hear

You want a clown
A clown
A clown to make you laugh he skips around
His face
A frown

You like the water
The water
The water always seems to get you hotter
The hotter
The water

You want power
Power
And power makes you louder
Much louder
Than the power

You want sympathy
Sympathy
But sympathy is only superficial
It lacks a certain
Empathy

You want to cry
To cry
And crying makes your body release endorphins
Which get you high
You like to cry

You want the best
The best
The best is always better
Than the rest
Because it's the best

Idle Pursuits

Salutations
To the cosmetically propped
Whose sagging flabby flesh is kept aloft
By tubes and wires
That bulge through fabricated sack cloth
All these lonely people

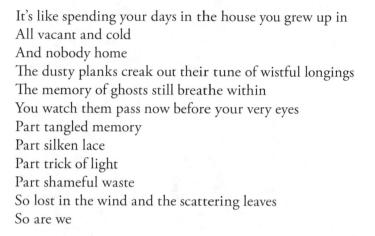

Hauntings

It's like spending your days in the house you grew up in
All vacant and cold
And nobody home
The dusty planks creak out their tune of wistful longings
The memory of ghosts still breathe within
You watch them pass now before your very eyes
Part tangled memory
Part silken lace
Part trick of light
Part shameful waste
So lost in the wind and the scattering leaves
So are we

We bear the brunt of our legislative minds
Our cold calculating minds
It's like the carnival of swirling lights
Excitingly thrilling moon drenched nights
That one day
It all passes seamlessly away
Now
Looking back into the rusty sunset
With unequivocal tragedy and remorse
You tell yourself that those were the days
As only they could be of course

So stands the tower of my youth
A home on the range
Fraught with whim and whimsy
A mixed blessing of bludgeoned dreams
Darkly kept secrets
Still so disturbingly beautiful
Still so morbidly entrancing
A specter of history that seeps and creeps forward as a living fog
Caressing you from the barren streets of a gutted out ghost town
The feeling of always being somewhere in-between the living

And the deceased
What is gone
And what is to come
I can only stare out into the air before my eyes
Felling the passionate darkness within
Perchance to cry

The Daughter of Desires kisses me lightly
As she catches air to distant realms
In that moment
So easy to slip
Yet I draw into the inner circle
And so do you
As I turn away from what we now have become
I will most certainly sneak a glance back
Someday soon
We will pass this way again

Fare

All your friends must come to you
With the rising of the Moon
You've got all your friends and they come to you
With the rising of the Moon
Silently
You close your eyes
You close your eyes to light
Silently
With retrospect
Younger than the youth
You don your sweet disguise
All of you
Gone underground
Always underground
In all of you
No love be found
No fear be ever found
Consuming breathless air

Agitated fantasies
Of those too cold to care
Introspective callousness
Alleviates your fears
It happens

To breathe the air
To breathe in shallow air
It happens
So watch yourself
Consuming breathless air
The dank and crispless air
All of you
Try not to hear
Try not to hear the words
In all of you

Crisp conscious clear
With night you reappear
Then fade into black
And with the morning breath of life
You slowly disappear

Exquisite Temptation

The Jester
In all his subtle wit
Brought me here to this dreamscape room
Cologned in pillows and perfume

The sweetness of naked skin
She lay there now
A beautiful creature of exquisite temptation and maturity
So pleasantly fine
She is many women
Yet she is one
Mother lover daughter sister
Wife widow woman whisper
She's a plausible past
An improbable future
She is here and now
Her skin against my groveling lips
Nylon silk and creamy milk
Her small firm breasts rise and fall gently
With the movement of her breath
She is cooing and caressing
Opening herself completely to me
Writhing and arching rhythmically
I am surely rust and ruin
Clumsy in my cavorting
For I am crushed with rapture and want

And the Jester?
Why he's crouched in the corner
Insane and pallid
His grin stretched like tissue over bone
In immaculate madness

Ethereal Blue

To feel your cool flowing depth
Caressing over and around me
Tingling my skin
My hair standing on end
Goosebumps blemish my outstretched arms
My dangling legs numbing without weight
Sending shivers up my spine
To alight playfully
Upon my scalp

To touch your wispy white passengers
Who continuously shift in shape and shade
That color the day
And are colored by its close
In their cluttering contrasts I am captivated
Entranced by their gentle
Gliding grace
Lost in thought and unaware
I am there

To experience your beauty
Natural and unrefined
Would release in me more of what is you
Than to witness
Could ever satisfy
Speak to me ethereal blue
Let me listen to your lingering lull
Slowly sweep me to your dizzying heights
Where weightless
My heart may swell

Edge of Night

Within my soul
A humble glow has gently formed
But what I see is
A brush of fog
Upon a swath of sky
And quite beyond
No...
Distant
Gone
A glinting pin of light exists
Sailing in the astral pit
With countless things beyond imagination
Or what little known

And there resides my soul
Emitting mood and inspiration
Sentiment for photographs
With a lustrous marveled breath soon passed
For ruined homes
And vacant tones
For sudden flickering days
Once shone
A past that never dies

But matters of such nature
As so previous in stone
Hold no gulag for this edge of sky
And its nebulous abode
As ever now soon sheathes the evening
Summer creeps from under covers
Convoking all that lay await
Which no one knows a scratch about
Seems past is tucked away in ink

And aging photographs
Of the times to never be again
That memories control
Lie always to be seen

Cipher

Thoughts are dreams you cannot see
And you can't see the thoughts in me
If I disclosed those dreams to you
They wouldn't be thoughts at all
Anymore
They'd be messages and clues
That once deciphered
Would reveal with clarity
My thoughts in truth
Which are really only feelings
Deep and blue
Feelings for you

Carnivores

Vultures gleaning
Ripping
Grasping
Madmen laughing
Laughing
Laughing
Summer yawning
Fading
Dying
Children sighing
Crying
Crying

Carbonation

You've cosmetically enhanced
Your bubbly personality
You drain it from a bottle
And it fizzes in your head
You're unafraid now
To blend into the infinite crowd
It suits your brand new image
Like skin around muscle
But that's a façade
Because yours is really like plastic
Stretched pathetically
Around the aluminum and artificial eggplant substitute
That comprises your bulk
Others must be blind
Unable to see it squish about unpleasantly
Beneath your desultory exterior
No sweat leaks from your pores
And your hair always seems to stay fashionably in place
It makes me wonder if you are real at all
The cheer upon your face looks painted
Different shades for different days
To compliment your skin tone
If in actuality
Skin exists beneath it
I can't tell
If I wasn't any wiser
I'd say you were a mannequin
I'd find you a job as a store display
Looking prim and lovely every day
But that may change your lively mood
And even that seems tired
And used
Still
You really got the life in you
You're so socially adept

Always looking new and fresh
Though it seems there's a production line somewhere
At an enormous manufacturing plant
In a dreary
Malaria riddled third world country
Where gnarled hands
Cracked and split and leathery
Toil dawn till dusk
For a bowl of spoiled rice
And a cup of brackish water
Making carbon copies
Of typical you
Still they do make your clothes
That truly exquisite designer thread
That is all the rage this season
Feed the wheel

Even your water
Contains carbonation
And bears a name
Your composition
Is sadly the same

Blue

Fine hair
Bright eyes
Dark trees
Ash skies
Wind calls
Leaves dance
Owls screech
Footsteps
Branch creaks
Wings flap
Whispers pass
Eyes dart
Hands search
Fog parts
Mist laughs
Clear tears
Lost lives
And eyes
Blue
Blue

Apples to Ashes

In a lifetime full of madness
Curtains close upon each scene
And through the looking glass of past mistakes
We see what might have been
Putting peanuts in your pockets
Pushing pennies down a drain
Coinage filters through the markets
As do all our dreams

We know all too well
That we can be that pale

§BLACK FLY§

"There is no coming to consciousness without pain."
~ Carl Jung

Introduction to These Thoughts

In a lifetime full of madness
Curtains close upon each scene
And through the looking glass of past mistakes
We see what might have been

For when your thoughts blister and bubble with cheap eccentricities
        Like brie on a lard laden griddle
For when the cheapness of your darkened soul worries and troubles
        Over insignificant idioms
For when a horrific storm tramples the higher plains of your
consciousness on a violent rampage
        Leaving in its wake a suffocating residue of chaos
For when your hands quake and wither from the intensity of the moment
For when sores and boils blossom upon your upper extremities
        Festering on your shame
For when you feel compelled to grovel at the feet of insecure relations
        Licking their path clean with the ragged stump of your tongue
For when heartache and loneliness so consume your every waking moment
        That you obtain an overwhelming urge to strip and peel away your
        flesh in an effort to release the pain
For when everyone around you is distorted and strange
        And they all stare at you with curious sidelong glances
For when you perform questionable acts on yourself and others
For when the only words to describe the things you've done in your life
        Are nasty and dirty
For when everything comes together
        And your brain explodes with the madness of understanding
For when you feel nobody understands

These words in your hands

For when you cry all night long
        Wishing they could see
        But not really

Entertain Me

There was a time when I was needed by you
For whatever purpose eludes me now
But you requested my affections
And I gratefully obliged
So days cascade around us
Though those wounds will never fully suture
I've written thoughts about you
I'd like to show you when those scars have faded
If I'm afraid to find the lesson
It simply indicates I've found no teacher
Pray for me in solitude
When the heavy air seeps through your spine
I'll still remain subjectively
Within your tainted mind
Repeating scenes from life again
Forever and a day
Please entertain me
Never fade away

I'm sure this has happened to you
>Or rather

You might've been a part of it all
Passing it by as your soul measured distance
Across marbled tile floors in a sound garden hall
Across weather whipped asphalt or weed cracked concrete
Across a pebble littered rock strewn shore
>While the tide licked your ankles

>And the salty mist gathered on your tongue

Across copper wires that crackled like snapping bones to foreign destinations
Across a barren wasted landscape with a scattering of ancient trees
>Dead and twisted with agony

Or perhaps it was a crowded room
>Loud with plaster masks and empty dialogue

>To the upstairs floor

>Where behind a door

>You padded cat-like across a plush carpet

>To a swollen bed

Or maybe on an open grazing pasture
>Where the flies gathered thickly about the putrid piles of cow fodder

>As creamy wisps of clouds smeared their way along the currents of a dead blue sky

You might've been a part of it all
Recognized a facet or two
Or experienced an even deeper blue
But this is for those who've known it all
Who've seen what's really there
And will recognize its guise
Until the last one left confides in death
Let's read about despair and love
Life
And its demise

Wheat

I am standing in an endlessly open field
Of this I know not where
The spectral blue sky looms above
With thunderheads afloat afar
Battleships in a glassy sea
Wheat
In flowing stalks of grain
Greet the infinite horizon
Swaying to and fro
Rippling in lazy waves to the ever bidding breeze
The wheat
Tickles my neck
Teasing it like a thousand caressing fingers
It's all so very beautiful
Quite a breathless take
Magnificent
Grand
Bold
Lonely
So very lonely
Consumed in overwhelming thought
A buzzing hits my ear
Slight at first
But caught with growth
Spinning like a lumbering ball of fire
Till at last it tumbles by
Roaring with thunderous applause
Bursting in my ear
And thronged in grope
I shrieked and flailed
Thrashing off the bed sheets
And setting sail the smitten clock
To shatter against the wall
Unobtrusively
It resigned to the floor

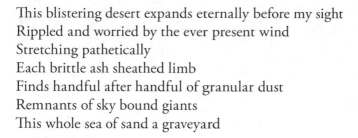

Black Fly

This blistering desert expands eternally before my sight
Rippled and worried by the ever present wind
Stretching pathetically
Each brittle ash sheathed limb
Finds handful after handful of granular dust
Remnants of sky bound giants
This whole sea of sand a graveyard

Days of hours of minutes flow past this waste of memory
Now a gnarled skeletal sentinel
Creeps gradually towards me
Twisting and writhing in this liquid heat
Its crooked strips of shade beckon me to a microcosm of relief
Still the air is sandpaper in my throat and lungs
My chest burns like a furnace
And my cracked papery lips tremble uncontrollably for moisture

The fire in the sky
Drapes its boiling blood upon this desert
As I bake within the gradual shade of this marrowless and bent tree
With my soul seeping into the life sucking grains
Should I savor this intensity?
This piss pale sky engulfed within my eyes?
But now the tickle of tiny legs with stiff sharp hairs prickles my nose
And my eyes cross sharp to focus in
A black fly's gaze returns in multitudes

I've visited this barren land a thousand times before
And every time I've reached this tree
Whose own weight bears it down
Yet still it bears the brunt of me
And every time this black fly comes
And lands upon my shredded nose
It stares me down
Rubbing its legs in anticipation

A hundred eyes judging me
Feeding on my weakness
Waiting for that last listless breath
To savor the sweet meat of despair
And death

Look Away

Stare at me you all
Stare with hesitation
Then quickly avert your gaze
Avoid the flush that floods my cheeks
My breath turned stinking hot
From the rancid paste of fear and failure
That thickly coats my swollen tongue
The traitor that places me
Within such states
Such situations of dread and social angst
That slick slug of caution
Deliberates with the hunkered mind
Which cowers and quivers with an ineptitude of grace
Carried by those whose pirouettes rank style

Inside me it is so clear
Crystalline like childhood
As expressive as my troubled youth was intense
Run with reckless fancies
Grandiose schemes
And brutally faithful love
That now still burns deep within
I wish you could join me there again
Without the ribbon-like madness
Or the twilight trim
Where I could keep the weakness of my soul
Within me
You could visit when you wanted
But now I'm cast upon the arena
And it has worn upon my face
In the embarrassment of inexpression
From a sluggish stumbling tongue
I beg you not to gawk in idle
I beg you
Look away

A Day to Dance

Give to me this moment of solitude
To tranquilize this troubled heart
To soothe these weathered nerves
And quietly console these open memories
Half-healed wounds
Ulcerated sores
And simple scars that cease to pain
Let me be myself
To stand outside with my face turned high
Allow the rain to cascade casually over my skin
From the bruised and battered sky
Let me collect again
My wits about me
If wits be there to gather
And breathe the sweet perfume of misery
That urges my existence

Give to me this day to dance
To celebrate and smile
To adorn myself with soft attire
And revel in absolution
Let me tumble and twirl and glide and flip
Without critique or laughter
Let the dance be elaborate
And the joy be simple
For I have witnessed the restitution of my spirit
From the burdensome grievances
My lifetime's endured
Old acquaintances are fresh again
Shrouded in excitement and mystery
Bludgeoned by desire
Let my presence engulf this day again
Lift my heart so I may fly

Take from me this deflated world
This gracious field of lost horizons
And panic strewn dreams
Press into my palm two coins of copper
So that with these withered writhing hands
I may lay waste to what remains of my dignity
And embrace the soil again

Rain

Face of wax
Seen dripping through the window pane
Its silhouette pattern
Stained upon my cheeks
Creeping up behind me rising on the wall
I am larger there too
In that nebulous state
Trapped in a tenuous existence
Playing to the whims of light
As I lurch and lurk to avoid exposure
A marionette shifting and twitching to the oscillating brightness before me
Yet I am still
Even the light is wax
As it strikes the wall it drips
Melting into my shadow substance
Cascading down in rivulets upon the glass before
And behind
But the glass it sparkles
It melts like liquid crystals
With dazzling flecks of gem
And as my eyes defocus
It turns to streams of rainbow snowflakes
And the light outside grows wider
Yet I am still
As my hand supports my chin
With my elbow upon the windowsill
And the cavernous thoughts that occupy the recesses of my mind
Drip like mud
From the warmth and hope that is the light
Into the shadows cast by what is night
And the barrier before me
Between the brightness and the window pane
Increases evermore
To rain
And I am still

Autumn

Autumn leaves
Crackle and fold
Full of fiery brightness
October breezes
Chilly and bold
Our shadows blown steeply behind us

They gathered around the table
With their hemlock lips
And ivory skin
Eyes peering through lengthy swaths of thread
Scribbling and scrawling
And furtively gazing
At the blistering crowds caught up in irony and deceit
Grabbing for friends
Grabbing for feeling
Grabbing for money comfort and dealing
Grabbing for answers and hopeless pursuits
Grabbing at trappings
So removed from the truth

Their lips peeled back in immaculate snarls
Through the reflection in their eyes
We've had enough
We've had enough
Inside their fingers trembled
Clumsily caressing
As they drew in each other's breath for sustenance
And all the while
As I stood in the background
Peering out from the wallpaper
They did not move
Nor make a sound
They simply watched and waited
And measured their minds with paper and ink

They begged and borrowed and stole
To fill the ragged hole
Now the paper flag is worn thin
And we won't let you in
The dealer of dolls wet his lips
The table maid squandered her chips
From all around us a din
That little voice creeping in
Grabbing hands
Grab all you can
Grabbing hands
Grab all you can
She scrawled mad as she clamored within
After all
It's a sick world

The brittle leaves
Swept up by a crisp wind
Swirled about them
Black clothed figures walking
Through a pallid mist

Inner Deviation

You come
And go
And come
Emerging from the darkness
To kiss me full upon the lips
Those full crimson pools reach out
From that white white face
And then you go again
Vanishing into that absence of the senses
That ominous nothing
Just beyond grasp
But when you come you are a dancer
With your flowing skirts of presence
Setting precedents for others
Who shadow every foot step
And yet I see you dance alone
Spilling grace upon the unfinished wooden floor
All eyes are upon you
But only mine dare not to speak
For somewhere in the silence that surrounds me
Within my blue blue eyes
Is the strength to resist you
How desperate my feelings resound
How lost they have become
You are a constant breeze
In a dual direction
Blowing through my window mind
I wish you would settle in some distant sorrow
Than reside within my brain
For I get meek
Shaky and weak
I really want to feel that way
And I really really don't

Smoothed hand
Willowy grasp
Traced ears
Supple laugh
Guided palms
Provocative hips
Subtle press
Mouth to lips
I am destroyed

Promise me you'll stay tonight
Let me glimpse your secrets
I've been sheltered by a guiding light too long
I know once you were flesh and bone
And immersed in tender trepidations
Now you are wrought and framed in silver
And warped by saline tears
The years
The years
The years

Masque

He huddles alone
In the wings of a darkened theater
Arms wrapped tight around his ribs
Trembling convulsively
His nails penetrate his costume
Gripping into his pallid flesh
So thin and frail
Talons clutching a kill
Bits of bone chip from his chattering teeth
As his lip dribbles spit to the tip of his chin
And an icicle sweat streams down his cheeks
His beautiful eyes dart hither and fro
From their cavernous twisting sockets
Those scary powerful eyes
Mad with intensity and emotion
As he cowers and quivers
And shivers with rabid fever
And inside his shuddering cranium
His brain twitches and squirms
Like a bucket of worms being scorched by live wires
His mind declares from a widening crevice
"iseeyouallinaswirlingpitandi'msickofitalljustsick!"

But on the outside he just smiles
And smiles
And smiles

Dark

Dark
Like blindness
Eyes wide
Straining
Big and round and bulging
Like they could just pop out
Vanish to someplace unseen
Arms outstretched
Fingers splayed
Nothing
Just wide open empty space
No
Something tangles my feet
Large and soft
A blanket
Wrap it around my naked body
Rock back and forth
Dark
And I am cold
I want to be held
I want to hold on
Emotions unraveling
Drifting away
Gone
Then come the nightmares
Garbed in deception and lies
Yet guised with familiar faces
Familiar settings
The struggle rends my very soul
A towel please
Any towel
Stifle the blinding white scream
Never mind
Won't emerge
Feebly squeaks through petrified vocal chords

Dribbles through my lips
A warm puddle on the floor
Doesn't end
Just passing through
Part of it remains
Tucked away in a distant rift
To gather potency
Visit again
Dark

Orange

I remember when the universe was only 50 feet in diameter
And I was smack dab in the middle
The only problems were the ones before my eyes
Behind me was forgotten space

I remember when my Dad was always in his Forties

I remember feeling unburdened and free
Utterly happy

I remember when the day went on forever
And everything was big

I remember when change was gradual
And I could keep up

I remember when I could close my eyes

I remember getting all worked up over nothing

I remember getting all worked up for nothing

I remember punishing insects for the crime of existence
And in an angry crimson heat
His blood pumping like magma
Molten sweat oozing across his brow
My Father did the same to me

I remember allowing my heart to openly bleed
Then suturing it up with barbed wire when nobody responded

I remember searching for love
As a physical need

I remember slicing my wrist
Observing it bleed

I remember passing valuable moments with friends
Who kept a constant eye on my back
To ensure that the knife remained in

I remember dancing alone inside a mirror
Grand sweeping gestures
Such grace
And the snow would tumble about me
I'd catch it on my tongue

Iremememberthingsaboutmyself Ihopenobodyeverknowsandthosewhodowill
notrecallactionsthoughtsdreamssoprivatemymindwouldshatterinhumility
ifevertheywererevealed

I remember feeling forlorn and distant for most of my natural life

I remember when my blue eyes were icy
The color of steel
And just as hard to read

I remember giving in
To an unforgiving need

I remember when Jesus Christ
Answered my prayers with pain

I remember tasting warm lips
Already drenched by rain

I remember quite often being unable to express myself
Either physically or mentally
And possessing no means by which to define my presence in this world

I remember taking it out on myself

I remember using my family and friends
And feeling remorse

I remember feeling no remorse and worse

I remember digging the graves
Clawing maniacally at the soil
Hurriedly scraping with my fingers
Tearing my nails to bloody strips
Lungs screaming wickedly for oxygen
For I couldn't escape from the one I was in

I remember visiting a white room
Under lock and key
For feeling too much at any given time
All anyone did was talk and talk
All I could do was cry

I remember the hot spray of water beating down upon my small frame
My head hung low
Absorbed with the drain
Rivulets trickling furiously down my chest
Tickling my loins
And that dark intent so alive behind me
I tried to be my best
Forgive me

I remember the calm before the storm

Vein

You come to me through mirrors
Each reflecting an appearance
Your magnetism besieges me
My vision strained
With inadequacy

You straddle me with pleasure
So I long for your acquaintance
You entice and tease my senses
My consciousness reels
My body drains

You promise me a fortune
That is spent with your arrival
My dignity remains silent
As it ebbs ever dimmer
And I am lost

You enter my head
Like a gathering storm
A hurricane of images and emotions
Brewing and boiling to a climax
Take me in your potent arms
Embrace my wretched frame
Make me live
Make me live again

Nightscapes

I don't want to go to sleep tonight
That ancient mood has encroached upon my presence again
Twisting my grin
And guiding my hand to the pen
Allowing the perpetual flow of consciousness
To course through my veins
As my grey matter jitters to abate an ever pressing rictus
And within that fragment of indecision
Where neither side holds sway
I am so alive
I am high
My fingers dance in frenzy
My lips distress divine

Monsters

Seething jaws
Teeth bright and gleaming
Feeding on fear
Screaming
Screaming

Burdening memories
Crash upon me in waves
And recede in ripples
They dwell between the realms of bitterness and melancholy
Somehow sentimental
Strangely romantic
And still I exist
How do I exist?

I lay far and away
So stealthily dreaming
Avoiding their gaze
So hideous and wide
Day after day
They puncture new ground
And relish the feast
Of flesh they've worn down

Reality
Gradually poisoning my sight
Swarming wasteful needs
The numbers claw towards the light
A song of discontent
Violins so strange within its silence
Should I cry?
I cannot cry
My tears have bled to dry
And I am dying
Yet I cannot die

From behind insignificant borders they emerge
Descending upon vulnerability
Granite facades fail to display
The gnashing teeth
The ragged talons
They employ a breath before the kill

You may find them in your house
Stealthily secure within the suffocated shadows of accumulated possessions
Grinning enticingly with decadent offers
Hope and trust in dusty coffers
Our bodies unclean
Dirty
Obscene

I see my face in your eyes
You see my face as a child

Desolation

She owned a pocket gorged with strange dreams
Entombed within
Were all her earthly passions
Intensely searing evenings passed
Alone she wept in vain
The man of desecration came within her virgin frame

She gripped a trinket bright with strange dreams
Empowered within
Were all her dark obsessions
They adorned a veil of lace and white
And dwelt just below the surface
The man of desperation came to initiate her fears

She grasped a poem rich with strange dreams
Enshrined within
Were all her secret longings
They overlapped her sullen grief
And caused her deep distress
The man of desolation came and wiped her tears away

Pure

Pure
Is all I want to know
Like the brittle falling leaves
Upon the long green grass
Like the fingers on my face and through my hair
From a breeze gently passed
Or the absence of the hours
As I stroll a floral field
Or the sustenance of slumber
Where the landscape bleeds surreal
Like an icicle drips
On the white white snow
All I want to know
Is pure
Press your lips against my skin

Pure
Is all I want to feel
Like the tender touch
Of a childhood friend
The way her eyes reflect the evening sky
The way I tumble deep within
Or the fur of a kitten
Sweetly soft glides the skin
Thin swiftly flips a playful tease
Needles and pins
Like the rain cascades down
That prickly appeal
All I want to feel
Is pure
Press your lips against my skin

Pure
Is all I want to be
In the afterglow of laughter
Where the smile quietly quivers
Or the silent flow of consciousness
The swiftly swirling river
Bedded down within the carpet
Of dew lapped forest moss
Left to total isolation
My soul pleasantly lost
The consistency of motion
Like the shifting churning sea
All I want to be
Is pure
Press your skin against my lips

Animals

We are creatures of the night
You and I
Demons of projected flight
Leathery wings outstretched and wide
Hearts blackened to the pitch
Of the harboring naked sky
Iced air chills our lungs
In this sensuous dance
Our bodies a tangle
Silhouettes in the moon
Alone in a room

Candle flame
Candle flame
Flickering bright
Jittering shadows divide
Within the filtering light
You leaned in near
To touch my brow
I lost you there somehow

We are animals of deceit and shame
Paired liars
Bound to our quest of fortune and fame
How our hollow acquisitions remain
Pale
And bland to the eye
Through wispy veils our fears revealed
Our substance shone as intangible
The remaining vacancy within that brittle shell
Mirrors our discontent
We are not real

Jackal
Jackal
In the sweltering night
Fornicating within the steamy shadows
Of a sickly sweated alley
Beyond the sodium arc glow
Your tenuous laughter
A scream

We are creatures of the rain
You and I
Liquid in our impulses
Fluid in our motions
And wet with desire
As we cascade blindly into passion
Intensely we fall
Hurtling toward the inevitable
To break apart and lose ourselves
In the earth
The hardened earth

Sweltering Haiku

Soft transparent lace
Damply clinging to her frame
On this hot hot night

Sweet perspiration
Beaded pearls adorn her flesh
Gathered by my tongue

Hair falls about me
In whispery silken sheets
Gently tickling

Tenderly teasing
Her lips sprinkling petals
Velvet on my skin

Breasts heave full and smooth
Liquid heat consumes the mind
Breaths gasping as one

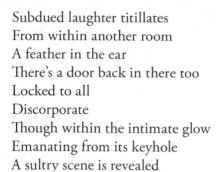

White Room

Subdued laughter titillates
From within another room
A feather in the ear
There's a door back in there too
Locked to all
Discorporate
Though within the intimate glow
Emanating from its keyhole
A sultry scene is revealed

Two slender sprites engaged together
Their shimmering sheets of midnight hair
Teasingly caress neck and shoulder
Starkly contrasting their creamy white flesh
Scarlet lips slightly part
Moist and full
Sensual
Serpent-like their tongues entwine
Hands gracefully grope
Beneath bridal veil skirts
And transparent lace tops
The pertness of their milky bodies
And the wicked ecstasy of their movements
Do not go unseen
I'm embarrassed by their inhibitions
Yet I cannot look away
A lustful shame washes over me
Yet in the keyhole's light I stay

They abruptly pause
And glance my way
Their ebony eyes sparkle with mirth
Aware of my presence
My desire
My angst

They resume their embrace
Relishing the attention
From within and without
This provocative moment continues to chill
So safe
And locked away

Rage

Blood fills face
Face burns hot
Fingertips pulse
Cranium throbs
Pounding
Pounding
Eyes blind white
Burning
Burning
A fury in the chest
A sun expands within the mind
Guts constricting
Adrenaline surging
Coursing through fibers
Popping every nerve
And with eyes of molten steel
Flaring nostrils
And sneering lips
A purge from the gnashing facial orifice
All the bilious filth
Guilt
Shame
Frustration
That should've emerged from the other end
And been flushed
In the all consuming porcelain whirlpool
Please excuse the display

To Be A Cloud

I would like to be a cloud
Unburdened by excessive weight
Or worrisome encounters
Free to merge or drift apart
To expand or contract
In company or isolation
To play whimsy to the Wind's content
To be without decision or destination
The sunset warm upon my mass
How uninhibited I would be
Yet graceful in my movements
To boil and brew in chaotic tempest
Electric and thunderous
When accumulation crescendos
Or to brood solemn and grey
Ponderous and full
Weeping without sorrow or pain
Or to loom large and white
Gentle and down
Wispy and light
Over sun soaked meadows
Green shifting swaying
Brimming with living complexities
Nonchalant in their surroundings
There I could be accepted
Unobserved
Nominally ignored
Yet there I would hang above the earth
Afloat on a manipulative stream of air
Observing all below me
Immune to the dictating regulations of time
And high in the expansive darkness of the night sky

I could stray peacefully between the curtain of stars above me
And the network of lights scattered across the black landscape below
There I could be free
I wish I were a cloud

Fatigue

Plumes of thick oily black smoke gradually rise from the scraped flat horizon
Against an ochre smog smeared sky
As smaller wisps permeate the discarded foreground
Amidst twisted shredded steel
Creeping wire barbed intermittently
Raped and blackened trees
And shrubbery
Dust
Dry bones
Spent tin cans
And chain
On this arid blasted landscape
Pay no mind to the agony left alive
Give it time
Give it time

Consumption

Paid a bill
Business completed
One less worry
One more pill
To ease discomfort
Assorted sizes
Various features
Child proof caps
Or not
I've got a choice
Beer is in the fridge
Grab one for me while you're in there
A sudsy rush
I've had enough
Yeah... we recycle
How much time do we receive for the return?
Never mind
Just don't leave the light on in the kitchen
What do you want?
What do you need?
There is a service
There is an answer
There is a handsomely chiseled young service representative in that particular department
Incredibly eager
Ecstatic to serve you
The air sucks away as you stroll into an expansive white room gorged with black clad masters and cheap imitation subordinates
Over here
Come with me
Take my hand and I'll light your cigarette
We can share a cup of coffee
It helps to wake me up
We won't use Styrofoam
It'll outlast humanity

Ceramic is a good second choice
But I digress
Look over there
That is the Doctor's office
He's got a lot of things that help save lives
And extend the one you've got
And over there another warehouse is being erected
To store all the lives the Doctor next door has saved
And extended
And right over there
Right over there
Is the last square foot of unexplored land on this Earth
A fence has been placed around it
In an effort to preserve its virginity
Come over here
There's a patch of soil
Where I've planted a garden
Roses and peas
Violets and poppies
The ground is rented of course
But the plants are mine to keep
Let's go inside
We can turn on the television
We can watch peoples' problems on display for our entertainment
Or we can escape into a movie
A plotline reflected from our imagination
The place where our lives can be better
Or more exciting than they really are
If you want we could turn it off
We could go somewhere
The skies are still blue
If we make it past the city
I know how comfortable our conveniences are
We could find a field
To run and play in

But we have to be home before dark
There are obligations to attend to
We need to eat
If we want to live
So many of us want to live
Is this the way we live?

Atmosphere

I know about being consumed by atmosphere
I know the feel of silver dust on a grimy palm
I know about dreams fulfilled
And those denied
Yet guised in devious facades of tempting light
Esteem falsely heightened
The illusion of lucidity
Those dreams caught in a tempest outside the calm
An atmosphere of tumultuous rain
Acidic with venom
Boil the blood
Sedate the mind
Rape the wind
And whatever alleviates your bitter fears
Acceptance or rejection
No death tonight
Only flight reckless flight
Let the power in the atmosphere swirling about you
Infuse within your skull
Penetrate your sight
You can find it within your group of peers
Corporate lounges
Cliques and croquet clubs
Take your stylish social stance
Blind yourself from the reality at hand
Let the atmosphere consume you
Fortify the illusion

Alone In A Room

Lamp bleeds heavy and wide
Spilling its cone across its wood grain rest
Splashing over the edge of the desk
To weightlessly spread about the comforted bed
Whose slumber lay long and deep
Whose dreams indulge in wispy fragments
And are kept well fed
Whose visitor curls up warm in its center
Dramatic in the shadows
Yet soft in the glow
Mild and endearing beauty flows upon her skin
In rippling waves
Absorbed by her body
And radiating gently outward

From an enchanted jewel in her heart
There resides a magic in those glinting eyes
Sometimes dark
But always bright
As she brushes her hair playfully over the eager diary before her
Pages fluttering in the wake
Her secrets are revealed
And realized

At night she is the eloquent stranger
Gliding through the intricate network of illuminated byways
That compose the brilliant dew laden web of the city
Wild and alive
Free to fly
Game to the dance

By day she is the breaking morning light
Arcing over the capricious midnight skyline
Bold and pure
Innocence revealed within the glimmer of her iris

Her rose dusted lips captured in a gesture of faint humor
Where it's lurking

Alone she is the aching heart of an anxious young woman
A single tear track trailing down her flushed cheek
Tempted by the future
Guided by the past
Driven on the ever present
Waiting patiently for it to pass

But alas you are a fleeting dream
An alternative
Never come to pass
If only slumber could wash away the persistence of your alluring image
Captivation is an indelible trait

Will that saturated parchment
Remain forever undisclosed within your grasp?
Desires unfulfilled?
Memories and timid fears tucked safely away
Within the confines of a bound and woven sanctuary?
Apart from the bone and flesh of reality?
Let no man compromise that fiery hair
Those distant sparkling eyes
Let no man contort or confuse
Your richly meshed melodious song
For no man can delineate your inner workings
What you breathe is yours
And yours alone
In a room

Maturity

The façade of stability
That coated the adult life like the sheen of a quality high polished wax job
Drew in my longing admiration
Beckoned my floundering impatience
When youth held the deed and title to my frame
And when that ownership passed over to the controlling interest of time
That polished coat peeled away
Like so many layers of cheap and flaking house paint
Deceived too strong of a word
Misinformed too light
It lies somewhere between the two
In incestuous revelry
Somehow
I'll learn to adapt

Terrestrial Life

The streets are full busily squirming with fabricated faces polyurethane bodies and designer fashions hurriedly scrabbling they close in on themselves as they grapple for space as they push their personal paths forward glances lost in suspicious flickering or locked in stony grimaces at some isolated invisible horizon their thoughts tucked haphazardly away within the confines of their wallets purses briefcases ties lips pinched nostrils flared and everybody walking

Walking

Walking

Everyone caught in a panicky waltz elevating their pace to some unheard musical dervish mad with personality captured in conformity they can never see beyond their exterior shells see the numbers countless numbers hear the noise the din of silent desperation and the cacophony of stomping feet bustle

Bustle

Bustle

Toil boil and hustle witness the blackened sky the acrid sting of spoiled air the slime between your fingertips and the grime the grime that laminates those imported costly threads can you see how filthy it is but no you must go on scuttle on now back to the boisterous mob of swinging arms and legs the world needs more and more as we speak there are customers being born and born the numbers go on but you all would prefer to trample the streets to greet your empty occupations with half mast sleepy eyes deliver your vacant dialogue with your tidy consumer intellect or simply say nothing at all and just suck in more air all together now people

One

Two

Three

Breathe

The Garden

Still I come to this place
This garden of my labors
Where the bittersweet obscurities of memory reside
Not a vagueness in recollection
But an ambiguity of feeling
A powerful fragrant mixture
Of passions once flared
Of innocence undermined and lost
Of wistful fleeting dreams
Of desultory longings
Of ebbs and flows and humility
And fear
Amid the tangle weeds of desperation
Amid the bramble barbs of shattered hopes
And pained expectations
This lifetime of a thousand fold
Whose endless reels of recorded experience
Are repetitively conjured within my head
Invading the present
Perhaps a flaw in my structure
Or a malformed mechanism of survival
Still it yields unto me
The strength of laughter
When my foundations strain and buckle under its own debilitating
weight
And the promise of rain
When the pain of existence has parched even those indelible creeping
weeds
The tears still flow
Still cleanse and restore
And because of this
This resounding restitution of my spirit
Though it may sometimes linger excruciatingly

Though it recurs more often than not
Than even I care to entertain
Still I come to this place
This garden of my labors

Desert Vision

Feel the wind blow cool and dry
See the sun rise above the uneven horizon in a progressive pawl
Let the day begin

The clouds shuffle fluidly across the blue and ancient sky
High upon the desert plain
I roam upon un-trodden ground
Nobody has ever been this way
And if they have
They've left no trace
The blossoms of anxiety I used to tend
When I scampered along the corridors of civilization
Have long since withered away
Now
I only share space with my vagrant thoughts
And only the baking air is displaced by my presence
The varied desert life ascertains little threat from my footfall and shadow
The scalding sands are challenge enough
The scarcity of moisture the only incentive

A shallow film of dust envelops my exposed and reddened skin
Clinging to and absorbing
The perspiration that wells up from my tired pores
As if it were driven by a clawing thirst
And the hot wind blows steadily into my squinting eyes
The blistering sun trickles down between some distant hills
Let the day end

At night I make a fire
Desert fire
Hot and dry
Bright
Always large
Fierce and flowing
Always the same

Always alone
Deep
Enticing
Despite myself I reach out long
To touch the flame
Consumed
I call a name
The flickering licks of heat's essence
Twist and flip
Like a magnificent mane of undying hair
Whipped about by a fickle breeze
It reminds me of a name
A name I call

How empty I would feel
Without pain
Without fear
How would I understand what tranquility felt
Without these demons
Tainted as they may be
These desert dreams somehow comforting
Their comfort carries me

Time erodes eventuality
Too long I've shuffled through these wastes beneath an unforgiving sun
My mind and my body unrecognizable
Shaped by isolation and heat
But they are one
All that I've heard and seen
Felt and known
Has long dissipated into the gradually shifting sands
And is lost to me
Save for the name
That indelible flame
It shimmers in pools of frantic liquid fire

That scurries across the continuous horizon
A fleeting temptation
Eager to escape my approach
Yet passive enough to play upon my desire
That little game of give and take
Teasingly titillating
Maddeningly infuriating
I've given up the chase
Because when the Night pacifies the Day's intensity
The flame is mine
The name
Divine

You would never presume she could be so harsh
Watching her bend and stretch into the beckoning distance
The first step into that expansive untamed beauty
That endless wildly flowing warmth
And you realize down to the marrow of your very soul
You can never have her
You can never tame
The desert vision

Fire

Fingers
Slim
Delicate
Roaming
Inquisitive
Body
High
Firm
Close
Heated
Moving
Lips
Moist
Deep
Open
Natural
Beckoning
Hair
Plush
Full
Lengthy
Unrestrained
Alive
Fire

Water Logged And Seaweed Bound

Let me go on about a fish I see
When I call he doesn't swim to me
Staring blankly
Floating on his side
He simply drifts without a shred of pride
What could possibly be on his mind?
I can't imagine that he feels alright
But then again
I haven't moved much since I've been down here either

Idiot Brow

Stare out at the monsters
Stumbling in the streets
The shouters
The mumblers
How they talk to themselves
With mind numbing heat
They're so misshapen
And disheveled
Uneven
Bulbous
And they're practiced at social ineptitude
How ever do they get around?
It's hard to hear their honking groans
Their piercing squeaks
Their languid moans
Amid the quietly desperate clamor that might comprise their molten
features
Embarrassing
Yet almost funny
It's somehow difficult to hold back
To contain the tickle that threatens
To blast with holy terror
From our pinched and perfect lips
At the monsters on the streets
Look at their crazy hair
Frazzled and askew
That open mouth
That hanging jaw
It compliments those stupid vacant marbles
Below that sloping furrowed brow
How
How
How
Do they ever get around?

Every pocket book purse
Every store front converse
Every mannequin stance
Every deviant glance
Every window and wall
Every telephone call
Every magazine rack
Every feeling in lack
Every mirror
Every day
Surely must display
The cancer of darkness within

The Crow

The crow glares on
With its curved and glossy beak
Its stark and piercing accusatory gaze
Screeches forth from that razor maw
Its unrevealing beady eyes
Glare on

On the streets
It sees the people run amok
Each clinging to their worries
Like monkeys cling to vines
To avoid the fatal fall
Each worry
Is the most important thing in the world
Though each does little else
Than validate existence
And bestow a smidgeon of importance
To their vacant
Unimportant lives

And all the while
The crow glares on
Its ebony polished feathers
Unyielding to the blustering breeze
As each singular worry passes into diminished substance
Its eye remains fixed
Evaluating
It glares on

§ ARCHITECTURE §

"You can't crawl your way out of a pit until you realize you've fallen into one."
~ Scott Byorum

The world is pretty big without you
Lost are my thoughts
Lost my emotions

And can I really be without you?
How am I fraught?
Where are my motions?

The bed is a great expanse
Wide in girth and breadth
I feel confined to one edge for comfort
You are warmth and presence
A tangible vacancy

American Male

Happy with his job
Happy with his wife
Happy with his kids
Happy with his life

Happy making business deals
Happy stabbing backs with knives
Happy with his secretary's
Skirt above her thighs

Happy with his social buddies
Happy with his friends
Happy when he gets from them
More than he puts in

Happy with his finances
Happy with his plans
Happy finding loopholes
When he gets to stiff The Man

Happy with his country
Happy with his guns
Happy when the President
Has the bad guys on the run

Happy taking camping trips
Happy watching sports
Happy fixing up his house
And surfing online porn

Happy with his alcohol
Happy getting high
Happy when his eldest son
Can't look him in the eye

Happy when his wife is wrong
That look upon her face
Happy with his anger
When he puts her in her place

Happy with his daughter's smile
Happy with her friends
Happy thinking of their bodies
Naked touching him

Angels

Angel had a friend
An Angel deep in trouble
The distance in their friendship
Seemed to treble
And then double

Each Angel had a marble
That contained their true desires
Each Angel sat upon a cloud
Each cloud swept up higher
Higher

Angel lost her marble
It rolled off from her cloud
And to the earth below
Other Angel never pondered
Where her own marble would go

So Angel with a marble
Gave the ornament away
To the friend without possessions
And she took breath unto her wings
Without further delay

Angel found the precious orb
Within the architecture
Of the mortal mind
Witnessing their need for substance
She dared not rob them blind

Returning to her lofty cloud
She saw her friend
Secure within its fluffy charms
And Angel with the marble
Held another in her arms

Angel gave Angel the extra
Because it came from within
A piece of her heart
And it kept a measure of their distance
So they would never be apart

Architecture

This wall remains in position around me at all times
This wall barricades my thoughts from outer influences
This wall is tall and wide of girth
This wall has been erected gradually since my birth
This wall protects my eyes from unsavory characters and occurrences
This wall defines my space within its enclosure
This wall fortifies my heart sheltering it from harm
This wall sifts through and screens out all but the most favorable noises
and visions
This wall allows not for open arms or warm embraces
This wall is void of protrusions armaments or garrisons
This wall is sheer and indomitable
This wall emanates obstinacy
This wall is its own security
This wall secures its own reality
This wall requires enormous reserves of energy to maintain
And I have weakened

Bad Man

Bad man in a basement
Drunk
And full of fear
Naked in his musings
Using what is near
And still
He manages to rise

Bad man in the daylight
Drunk
With isolated thoughts
Dealing with disasters
Tying twisted knots
And still
He manages to lie

Bad man in the evening
Drunk
And delicate
Patterning his mysteries
On failings in the past
Dancing
Dancing
Spinning
Spinning
Pretty liquid ice

Bad man at the table
Drunk
And tense with tears
Scratching at the surface
Digging through the years
And still
He manages to smile

Bad man in the cradle
Drunk
And lost in fog
Mewling for his Mother
Father wrote the log
And now it's just a ledger
A tidy little Bible
For the bad man's latest song

Bad man in the bedroom
Drunk
And elegant

Balance

The balance of a smile
Through the haze of countless obstacles
Eases what we undertake
And there we build our trust

The arc of forming friendships
On the structure of our hectic lives
Gives order to the chaos
Brings patience to our minds

And though our days pass furtively
The past receding incessantly
No stranger than the air we breathe
Are you to me
Are you to me

We're building on foundations
With the counterweight of foresight
We're grasping for stability
Towards a tenuous future
In an unknown state
Yet it is always there
Within our reach
The balance of our smiles

Body Talk

Eyes
Eyes like webs that capture light
As a droplet's shine is twice as bright
Moistened lips part heart to sleight
Make it mine
Make it mine

I'm a fly in your attention

Thighs
Thighs to skirt shown long and high
Shapes above stretch fabric tight
Calf to heel taut muscles rise
Etching sight
Etching sight

How I work to serve for fiction

Cold Dark House

Alone on the couch
Stranded with the silence from the day's dark energies
Spent in nightmare
Such uproar
Such aggression
Such racket
Besieged this abode of trust and care and love
Bonds broken with brutal abandon
And now we suffer in separate silences
In this cold dark house

Remember laughing like children?
Remember innocence and intimacy?
Remember loving and being loved?
Remember?
How sudden the castle is razed to the earth
With storm clouds boiling across our irises
Is this all we are?
Mindless demons lurking to liberate their horror of fear and failure?
Or am I alone the perpetrator of this madness?
Are you the hapless victim?

The daymare approaches of having to face you
Of having to struggle to meet your eyes with mine
Of searching for something meaningful to say
To append and amend the meaninglessness of that day
And I am alone on this old couch
Listening to the forlorn wind of fear
That caresses the guilt and insecurity
That pervades my mind
Stoking a restless night
In this cold dark house

Father's Strength

I sought my Father's wisdom
I sought my Father's cheer
I sought my Father's loving strength
But all I found was fear

Worry that I did something
Worry that I didn't
Worry about my Father's worries
Worry about what isn't
Worry about the future
Worry about the past
Worry about how long I fear
This worrying will last

A child is seeking wisdom
A child embraces cheer
A child longs for loving strength
Without which blossoms fear

Locked within his journals
Groping through this maze
He seeks the path back to the womb
To avoid the mirror's gaze

The problem with Scott is not quite a lot
Not quite what you'd think of as wrong
His mind floats above
All he sees
All he loves
And his thoughts are a torturous song

The problem with Scott is he thinks quite a lot
And his thoughts are as deep as are long
His mind carries lies
The deceived
Where he hides
But his heart knows what really went on

The problem with Scott is he knows quite a lot
And he knows he will never belong
They all pass their way
From their birth
To their grave
And he stands outside safe gazing on

The problem with Scott is he sees through a lot
And his eyes view the past living on
In the shower's warm rain
Dark betrayal
Dark pain
And the act resonates like a gong

Ghost

Alive
They are alive
And they celebrate life
With their children
Who are their lives
You can see them in the parks
In the malls
In the nursery halls
They are social and serene
Frantic and obscene
They make pacts and share secrets
And consume the normal life
Before their eyes
Their children's eyes

I'm a poison in their reign
An outcast of the same
An outlaw to the norm
And I feel it
Oh boy do I feel it
It's a rising storm

Dead
I am dead
And I celebrate death
Without children
And in their eyes
I am a ghost in my car
On the street
That no one hurries to meet
I'm alone and serene
Frantic and obscene

I hide acts and hold secrets
And consume the normal life
Behind my eyes
My saddened eyes

Husband to one
Father to none
Caretaker of the abandoned
And I feel them
Oh boy do I feel them
They are an embracing warmth

Interwoven

There's little to speak of for the Rim World down here
That frantic sprawling wilderness of glass and steel and concrete
Where veins of pavement feed arteries of howling congested light
    Streaking through the nightscape like errant stars
Where a continuous conflagration of business is disturbed
    Only by brief pockets of pause for consumption
Where humanity rages in an expanding tide of frustration and exhaustion
    Eager to fill the passing minutes with vacant trivialities and banal
    tidings
Where each stranger dons a mask painted in varying shades
    Of false modesty determination and insecurity
    Clawing and clutching at trinkets of amusement
    As if each defined a portion of one's soul
    The spirit of which vacated the artificial wilderness of the Rim World
Long ago

It is a spirit which moves here now
Within these canyon walls
And it touches and binds us with each other and itself
And we are dwarfed by the elusive passage of time
That has now become overwhelmingly transparent
Here we grasp but a fleeting whisper
Of an ancient tale
Painstakingly etched in the multihued layers
Banded chapters of distant memory
That tower so dizzyingly around us
Here the minutes are years
The hours are eons
And lifedeathbeauty intermingle in a naked dance of fluid persistence
Something we can only appreciate from afar
No matter how close we get to it
The moment teases us
A time which we once knew so far from us now
So removed from the encroaching Rim

Never again will we witness the grandeur of today's sky
The clean perfume of the air around us
Untainted by our own desires
For there is a new sky in the making
Just around the river's bend
Paralleled by majestic spires and cathedrals
Of time-hewn earth
This temple which echoes the voices of the Old Gods
And for which we are a part of
Only in temporal unity

Kiss Me Kindly

Kiss me kindly
In the October wind
As the leaves play a dance
Against your hair and your skin

Kiss me kindly
When I've followed you there
And time fills the balance
Of our void in the air

Kiss me kindly
When I'm alive in your arms
Take me in your soul
Take me in the wind

You wear my heart on your skin
I wear your kiss from within
Your eyes glow in the dusk
Your hair swims in the wind
So kiss you
Kiss you I must

Legends

Legends of the gods are we
Martyred by morality
And cast amidst the elements of discord
The fire of their desires
The grandeur of what exists
Still
And since the very earth itself
Crawled up to crack and chafe
To breathe its life into boundless forms
It resides here still
In marbled temples
Chambers wrought majesty and silver
Worked in intricate gold fascinations
So in thought we are bold
Immersed in tragedy
And triumph
Paralyzed with passion
And love
Contagiously comic
On the theater stage that is our lives
It resides precariously on the borderlines
The netherworld
The profane
And it is there that we conjure our dreams
From the agony and the ecstasy
From the ashes within
From the dust of stars we are born
This is the doorway to our world
As its seasons cycle
And come whatever may
So too we
Will pass this way

There's a rug on the floor
And for a long long time the same Family walks upon it
Leaving a piece of themselves on it each time
Sometimes it's dust
Which tends not to stay
Sometimes it's mud
Which clings as it may
And sometimes it's worse
Which stains it that day

And the days turn to months turn to years

The Family's housekeeping is shoddy at best
But it needs to be done to hide the unrest
Everyone takes time to make the house clean
(*some put forth more effort than others*)
And the home looks pleasant and inviting
One of the tools they use to clean is a broom
It's guided by hand from room to room
It sweeps the floors
Piles up the dust
But at times the person gets lazy
And sweeps the little dust piles under the rug

And the days turn to months turn to years

Over time the rug starts to look dirty
Oh you dirty
Dirty little rug!
The person cleaning one day lifts it up to clean it and lo and behold
Just look at all the filth underneath!
Oh what a filthy
Filthy little rug!
Hoarding and hiding all that filth!
The rug is taken outside and shaken and beat
It's sprayed and it's washed to remove all the stains

(*but not all of them come out*)
After it looks clean it is put back on the floor
And the whole cycle repeats itself

And the days turn to months turn to years

After a time the rug looks coarse
And frayed
And tired
(*some are better woven than others*)
So it is thrown in the attic
Or the garage
Or the garbage
Replaced by new rugs
And wherever it ends up it collects more dust
And dirt
And filth
And worse
Overlooked
Forgotten
Unraveling

And the days turn to months turn to years

Mr. Bones

Mr. Bones and I stay up late nights
Just sittin' around
I sit on the couch and stare at him
He sits in the chair by the window
Just starin' out into space
Right out into the heart of the galaxy
Heavy stars out tonight man
Heavy stars!
And I drink a beer and think
Then I have another one
And I read a couple paragraphs from a book
My favorite author wrote it
But he ain't sayin' it
I'm readin' it!
It's a story
But it's crazy man
I don't know where it's goin'!

I can see outside too
Right out into the goddamned street
And the wind is blowin' out there
Blowin' right on down the street
And there are leaves flyin' out there too
Flyin' leaves man!
And these thoughts man
These thoughts are all squishy inside my head
Like butter

And all the while I'm thinkin'
Where's this story goin'?
And all the while I'm thinkin'
Dig that crazy Mr. Bones!
And all the while I'm thinkin'
That wind is freakin' me out man
And all the while I'm thinkin'
I gotta get to bed man
I gotta get to bed

And Mr. Bones is sittin' in that chair
With a big ass freaky grin on his face
Just frozen there like a stiff margarita with an extra shot
Hold the salt man
Hold the salt
Dig that crazy Mr. Bones

My Witness

You are witness to my best
The heart within my chest
And what I always seem to fail to see
You are witness to my worst
My loathing and self-curse
And what I always seem to fail to see

And still you stay with me

I will strive to see my quest
To view each day as fresh
And open up my heart to what will be
I will strive to end my hurt
To balance what it's worth
And open up my heart to what will be
So you will stay with me

Never Apart Or Alone

I stroll on the air when she's holding my hand
I float in the yard when she's home
I hide in my heart when she's absent from me
I drown in my thoughts by the phone
Now she's smiling and laughing and carrying on
I could break down and cry but I won't
We are lost in a world of our own
We are never apart or alone

The world around is a horrible place
Wrought with war and disease
And when we get caught in that terrible maze
That sick complication of needs
I kiss her soft lips to make sure she's still real
She brings herself close and I know
We are never unsafe or alone
We are one and the same and our own

On The Wind

I like a place where I can see
Trees cavorting in the breeze
Until I gently fall asleep

I like a place where water ripples in even rings
Where birds respond to love songs
Dancing with their wings

I like to hear all of the sounds
When nobody is talking
When all the artificial things in the world
Are silent

I like to be in a place
Where I know not the way
Like a desert or a forest
Or the endless breaking waves

Languid days
Passive nights
My heart beats tantamount
A living metronome
So pent up and wise
It smolders like a coal in the frost of my soul
Shy
Reclusive
Slight

Is this all that I am?
Is there nothing more?
There must be more
More to the mind than meets the hand
Or the eye can soon discern
More to the heart than makes the man
Or the fuel which makes it burn
More than what I tenuously share

With the other fragile beings and things
That live and turn
Down here

May I take this trifle thought
And gently blow it to the heavens
May the winds carry it forth
To a life unknown
That the gap in stellar loneliness
Closes one day
To our own

Once Upon A Time

The moon is dark
The sky is bright
Distant shadows warp the light

You were so thin
So beautiful
With your big white grin
And your thick red lipstick
And your friends

The sky is dark
The moon is bright
I see laughter
I hear lights

I was so thin
So beautiful
Elegant
I passed through the evening
And your friends
Like a rogue mist
To ravage your lips

I awoke within the mansion
The morning unveiled desertion of the monopoly
Yesterday's evening dance
Each room held sway over a lone reveler's slumber
And once upon a time
We slipped away…

Parenting Prance

Stick it in hard
Squirt them out fast
Raise them up and spank their ass
Put them in a crib
Fit them with a bib
When they wail you just ad lib

Make them walk
Make them talk
Make them dress and clean their mess
Pull their strings
They do things
Spread their feathers and clip their wings

Teach them right
Teach them wrong
Teach them how to get along
When they fail
Make them wail
And fret someday they'll go to jail

Now they're big
But they're still young
All their triumphs have been sung
Soon they'll burn
Soon they'll turn
They'll reach the days for which you yearn

Here they come
There they go
Back talk babies think they know
Days are long
They are strong
Never let them know you're wrong

Ship them out
Ship them fast
Time for once they watch their ass
Fix the house
Buy a car
Now you can unlock the bar

Some will win
Some will fail
Some will land their ass in jail
Some get stuck
Some get fucked
Time to find out who's in luck

This is called
The Parenting Prance
All through life you have to dance
And as you think
It's going to end
It's time to start it all again

Sunday's Song

A bottle full of tears
All the rage
All the pain
The agony
All the frustration
The temptation
The years
Fermented well
A taste of Hell

And this is Sunday's Song
With the vapid grey drizzle of afternoon waning to dusk
The river of consciousness flows by
Cathode rays
In a tube of dreams
The fantastic and the entertaining
The thrill of emotions
This is Sunday's Song

And how intense some things can be
Where you just sit and stare at each other
With uncomprehending ecstasy
The memories
Your face in an hour glass of colored sand
The patterns emerge on our weathered hands
Lives that map our whereabouts and where we were
With the speed of light we emerge in another time
Another place
Full of patience and fresh languages
Which dribble from our lips and tickle our teeth
Our tongues entwine
We are no more

The fabric of the day unravels into the unwoven night
Here I am with Sunday's Song

That Darkened Smile

That tingling hair
That sudden flush
That twitching cheek
That nervous stance
That flaring nose
That shortened breath
That heightened chest
That darkened smile
That darkened smile

Those gleaming eyes
Those timid lips
Those darting hands
Those trembling legs
That heated blush
That quickened step
That sidelong glance
That darkened smile
That darkened smile

The Cavern

I negotiate the craggy cliff
The salty mist assaults my senses
Tickling my skin and hair
Stinging my eyes
The tang alight on my tongue

And my ears are engorged
With the thunderous ebb and swell of the tide
My vision reels
Head spinning with light and shadow
The arc of the entrance before me
A gateway to the sea

I hug a rocky wall
Entranced by the weight of retreating waves
The pull of the mighty ocean
Moisture fused to all it caresses
Shivering with cold
I smile
I am so alive

The Dark Heart

The dark heart rises
Throbbing with barren promises
Again the silent speak of deceit
The presence known
The vision defined
Patterns unfocus and return to unrest
And all is lost in cold derision

The quiet heart emerges
Swelling with intensity
The brazen retire to frigid circles
Now clarity compels a voice
With unassuming strength
And verdant stride
Shadows disperse
The masquerade unveiled

The Dead Family

The weakness of the ring
And the depth of feeling
Pushing ever onward
And there's no more room to grow

The carrier of seeds
The creator of needs
The penetrator and the perpetrator
The looming shadow on the bedroom wall
Cowering inside
A child and his guns
The skin deep structure of the world outside
Teetering in his mind
And now
He is no longer just a boy

The maker of milk
The wearer of silk
The coddler and the martyr
The cowering shadow on the bedroom wall
Looming inside
A child and her dolls
The fabricated warmth of the world inside
Soothing in her mind
And now
She is no longer just a girl

Shall we examine the Dead Family?
Whose seed is stale
And impotent
Shall we interrogate the Dead Family?
Whose pregnant womb
Is circumcised
Potential life aborted
Shall we examine the multitudes?
The exponential numbers
The insatiable needs

Have pity on the Dead Family
And their best intentions
While we perpetrate our malignancy
Our conspicuous consumptions
Raping what we want from life
Family dead are we
As the dead family have foreseen
There is no more room to grow

The Little Things

It is difficult to focus past the daily murk
That which torques your attention to work
The little things
The inconsequentialities
The necessities
And the jerks
They all wrangle the mind
And in there they lurk

I long for clarity and simplicity
But I know I am the architect of my own complicity
I tangle with the brine
Let it muddle up my time
As my final destination races ever near
As days unfold to months unfold to years
Felicity belies stagnation

The Persistence Of Time

The most important events in life
The ones that enlighten
Or frighten
Or entertain
Or sadden
But inevitably change the way we view
And review life
And people
And the way things are
Our worldview
Are rarely realized at the moment they happen
Until the days
Months
Years
Have slipped insidiously and silently away
That is when you realize the potency and the change
The event unfolds in clarity and truth
You finally realize at that tremulous moment
That time
Truly does fly

The mundane moments in between
Get sucked into oblivion
The forgotten minutes of each and every life
Gobbled
By the persistence of time

Threshold

He stands at the Gate
On the threshold of thereafter
A man of honor
A man of horror
A man of love and compassion
A man of loathing and fear
Courteous and kind
Callous and careless
A pillar of strength and support
A well of unrequited wisdom
A burning photograph of despair
Insatiably insecure
Nihilistic
He is you
He is me
And he will stand there through time
At the threshold

Us

You and I
On the Autumn ground
In the brambly bushes
At the Junior College
By the constant sidewalk
Could they hear your soft moan?
My quiet cries of ecstasy?
Immaculate
We danced
In our tenuous leafy shelter
By the museum doors
We danced

And we fell as one
To the classroom floor
The air around us vacant of the day's lessons
Silent in the knowing
Chairs and desks
A neatly arranged still life forest
And we laughed
And we rolled
And we panted
Hoping the passerbyes would not come in
With the secret thrill
That someone would

And I took you down
Gently in the darkness of a paternal living room
The stereo lights and the soft music
Us

Wander

My ear is a hollow
Through which the wind mourns wistful tears
The leaves on the trees applaud
Their shadows rippling along the worn path ahead
Someone has been here
Someone has been here

My legs move
And I don't think
My arms swing
And I don't think
My lungs breathe
And my mind wanders
My mind wanders

A small lake opens up before my eyes
The way the plane of its surface continuously recedes
I could fall
I could fly
But it's only the wind
It's only the wind

Whistle Past The Grave

The New Year is like staring down the barrel of a gun
Cocked and ready to blast my mind into the next paraphrase
The erasure of time is upon me
Nothing ever changes
And Heaven has no name
And no conception in my brain

I want a life less ordinary
I want more time to make my story
I want the wind and sun to take me
Whistle past the grave
It's only seconds away

I want a world more ordinary
I want a simple happy story
I want to keep what I've created
Save me from the grave
It's always seconds away

Now I meet my morning glory
I see my whole life flash before me
What was once important now is not
Take away my pain
The seconds turn into rain

And unbeknownst to me the acts of others
Incomprehensible and inevitable
The erasure of time is upon me
God is always changing
But Heaven stays the same
A memory within my brain

World In Decay

Crawling out of bed
Head is full of lead
Bathroom lightbulbs shine and burn my eyes
Burn my eyes
First I gotta piss
Then I gotta shit
Neither looks to me like I've been wise
One day
To clear
My life

Driving off to work
Everyone's a jerk
Busy on the pedal and the phone
On the phone
Just a little late
Loathing and self-hate
Grate another day into my bones
One day
To be
Alone

A parting of the ways
A party to the grave
One might stop to think that I was blind
I was blind
My life was filled with lies
And now it's filled with nights
Soaking up the juice to make it right
One day
I'll make
It right

The world is in decay
Soon we'll have to pay
One day it will slip and pass away

Pass away
On the other side
No one is alive
Though some feel there's a light to guide the way
One day
I'll find
The way

About the Author and the Book

Scott has a BA in Psychology from Sonoma State University. He has always been interested in art, writing, and music and resides in Guerneville, CA, with his 2 Turkish Angora cats: Monkey and Flower.

All images in this book are original photography by the author, except the cover, which is Poseidon holding a trident, a Corinthian plaque, circa 550–525 BC, from Penteskouphia (photo by ©2006 Jastrow) and the inner title page, which is a Poseidon/Neptune sculpture in the Copenhagen Port, Denmark (photo by ©2005 Hans Andersen).

The concepts and ideas expressed in this book are of the author's interpretive imagination only, but based on his real experiences.